THE TOMB OF TIME

Luther Tsai has achievements worldwide as an architect, urban planner, author and academic. From creating spaces in the most vibrant cities of modern Asia, to creating innovative Humanities, Science, English and Mandarin curriculum worldwide – Luther and his wife, Serene Pang, the education consultant for this Series, recreate the remarkable Vision of Ancient China found in the Magic Mirror Series.

Nury Vittachi is an author based in Hong Kong. His writing is 'endearingly wacky', said *The Times* of London and 'heading for cult status' according to the *Herald-Sun* of Australia. Vittachi has had regular broadcasting slots on the BBC and CNN. 'Dr Who' star David Tennant recently recorded an audiobook version of a Vittachi tale.

For instructions to make a model of the Emperor's Army go to page 112.

Magic Mirror

Mysteries...

The Tomb of Time

LUTHER TSAI & NURY VITTACHI

SCHOLASTIC
New York Toronto London Auckland
Sydney New Delhi Hong Kong

Luther Tsai's dedication

Dedicated to my father who left to me the gift of dreaming and my wife Serene who helps make my dreams come true. With love to my two children T & T.

Nury Vittachi's dedication

To the children of Asia, who live in a region with a rich but under-celebrated history.

Illustrations by Durgadutt Pandey
Back cover photograph by prfctdayelise (under Creative Commons licence)

Published by Scholastic India Pvt. Ltd.
A subsidiary of Scholastic Inc., New York, 10012 (USA).
Publishers since 1920, with international operations in Canada,
Australia, New Zealand, the United Kingdom, India, and Hong Kong.

For information regarding permission, write to:
Scholastic India Pvt. Ltd.
Golf View Corporate Tower-A, 3rd Floor,
DLF Phase V, Gurgaon 122002 (India)

First edition: June 2012
This reprint edition: August 2024

ISBN-13: 978-81-8477-007-0

Printed at Shree Maitrey Printech Pvt. Ltd., Noida

What is Real?

What is Real?
In this story, facts and whispers of real life
people are here for you to find.
The rest of the story is made up of shadows and
reflections,
fleeting images of people and events that
remain, and haunt us still.

Look inside the Magic Mirror.

Imagine ... a Vision ... a Reflection ... Timeless ...
In the Moonlight.

There is a Place ... On a Mountain ...
A Mirror ... A Book ... and a Curse in the Wind.

Where can you find the mysteries of Ancient China?

Look inside a Magic Mirror.

'Now we see but a poor reflection as
In a mirror ... Now I know in part ...
Then I shall know fully, even as
I am fully known.'

1

Mysterious Lines

The doorbell rang. Neither of the two boys in the living room reacted. Thin, waifish Marko, still as a statue, sat reading a book in an overstuffed chair, legs draped fluidly over its arm. His left leg occasionally twitched. His short, chubby friend Virun lined up tiny soldiers into a platoon formation on a coffee table nearby.

The stillness seemed to have slowed down the speed at which sound travelled. Virun eventually glanced briefly across at his buddy. It was Marko's house, so surely it was his job to answer the door. But the smaller boy didn't move. Virun, a school friend who was visiting to 'do some homework', went back to his task, now re-arranging the soldiers into an attack formation. He assumed there must be someone else in the house, perhaps a servant, whose job it was to open the door.

Half a minute later, the bell rang again.

'Doorbell,' mumbled Virun.

'Yeah,' murmured Marko, not looking up.

'Shouldn't you answer it?'

Marko, engrossed in his text, looked up after two or three seconds. 'Huh? Oh, no, we don't answer the door. We almost NEVER answer the door.'

'What if it's something important?'

Marko, who had immediately returned to reading, once again took a couple of seconds to finish scanning a paragraph before languidly looking up. 'Hmm? Oh, we have a system. Whoever is upstairs checks the remote viewer thingy. If it's someone important, we answer the door. Mira's closer. She'll do it.'

Right on cue, there was a distant yelp from a female voice. It was an indistinctly shouted sentence of several words, apparently hollered from behind closed doors.

'What?' bellowed Marko at the top of his voice without moving from the chair.

The voice came again, this time a little louder, as if a door had been opened a crack. 'Can you check the viewer? I'm in the TOILET,' said his sister's voice. 'I'm going to be a while.'

The boy sighed. 'Okay,' he replied, reluctantly lowering his book. There was nothing he liked less than being forced to emerge from a book in which he had happily lost himself.

'Come on,' he said to his friend. 'I'll show you the remote viewer. I made it out of four periscopes and a torch.' He put his finger on his lips to indicate that they should be as quiet as possible.

The two boys scampered out of the room and up the stairs, stopping at the landing of the old house. The doorbell rang a third time, accompanied by a cursory knock, as they reached the viewer—a plastic periscope top set into the window.

'Postman,' said Marko. 'See?'

Virun closed one eye and peered at the periscope opening. He found himself looking straight down at a man in some sort of yellow and red uniform, holding a large soft bag with a shoulder strap. 'Hadn't you better see what he's trying to deliver? Before he goes away? It's probably some sort of special delivery. He's turning to leave. No he's not. He's getting out a pen to write a note.'

But Marko had leaned over to another mechanical device attached to the window –- this time some sort of speaking tube. He put his lips to it. 'Apologies for the delay. We will be right down to open the door. Please stay where you are. Thank you.'

The postman looked up to see where the sound was coming from.

The two boys raced down to the front door.

Flicking the locks open, Marko swung the door open to reveal a surprised delivery man holding a small package, a little more than a fat envelope. 'Special delivery, Speedypost courier, for Ms Miranda Lee and Master Marko Lee,' he said. ''s that you guys?'

'I'm Marko and this is Miranda,' said Marko, pointing to Virun.

'Shut up,' said Virun, slapping his friend's arm.

'I'm Marko, and Miranda is my sister and she's upstairs doing a poo.'

'Too much information,' laughed the postman. 'Any adults around to sign? The receipt should really be signed by an adult. Is your sister older than you?'

There was a distant flushing noise and a door opened. The three of them turned around as Miranda Lee appeared at the top of the stairs and walked grandly down.

'May I help you?' she asked, flicking water off her fingers. 'I am the lady of the house. I was just doing a, um, project upstairs.'

'Was it a big one?' Marko asked, giggling. Virun laughed too. 'Probably huge,' he said.

The postman, trying to keep his face straight, said, 'I need an adult to sign this.'

Miranda grabbed the pen out of his hand. 'I'll sign for it. I always sign.'

To the delivery boy she looked twelve-ish or maybe somewhere in her early teens, but definitely not eighteen yet. But after a slight pause, he decided to let her have her way. There was something bossy about her. You didn't say no to Miranda Lee. 'Well, okay, I guess that'll be all right, thanks Miss,' he said, taking the receipt back. 'Now you can get back to your project.'

She turned to the two boys, who were chuckling at the courier's words. 'What are you two laughing at, idiots?'

They shook their heads to signify that no answer would be forthcoming, and followed her as she went into the kitchen to get some scissors with which to open the letter.

Virun said, 'I meant to ask, how come you guys live by yourselves? I mean, like, how do you get away with it?'

'It's a long story,' said Marko. 'But basically our parents went on a trip and left us in the care of our grandpa. And at pretty much the same time, our grandpa went on a trip, leaving us in the care of our parents. They were due to return roughly the same time as he left.'

'So like each thinks you are being looked after by the other? Man, that's cool,' said Virun. 'You guys are SO lucky. Doesn't anybody check?'

Miranda said, 'Our parents are in a place with no phones, like Irian Jaya or the Amazon or somewhere. They do that sort of thing all the time. They did call a couple of times, but we said we were doing fine and they didn't need to rush home, so they extended their trip.'

'We didn't like it at first, but we kinda got used to it. They've been gone nearly three months,' said Marko.

'You've been free for three months? Wow. You are SO lucky. Your grandpa didn't come back either?'

Miranda went to get the scissors from a drawer while her brother answered the question. 'Grandpa used to be a historian. He's supposed to have retired but he never stops. He goes around exploring and collecting old stuff. He's always on the road. And he's not a mobile phone sort of person. He writes letters and sends packages instead.'

'Like this one?'

'Yeah,' said Miranda, the tip of her tongue protruding from her mouth as she carefully snipped open one side of the package. 'It's from him for sure. I can tell by the writing.'

She pulled out a letter. Another piece of paper fluttered from within its folds.

Marko grabbed it. 'It's a poem,' he said, surprise in his voice.

'Is that it?' said Virun, disappointed. 'A letter and a poem?'

Before they could answer, there came the sound of a car honking. Virun went to the window, recognising the sound. 'It's my mom,' he said. 'I gotta go.'

He ran back to the room where they had been sitting to get his schoolbag. Less than a minute later, he was in the car and driving off. Marko stood outside and waved to him.

Then he raced back into the house to see what the letter said.

'Look. It's got an address this time,' Miranda said. 'And a warning. Grandpa says that he wants us to take the Mirror of the Moon somewhere. But he says we need to be careful, as there will be some "highly dangerous characters" about.'

Marko, who was nervous by nature, shivered. He didn't like the sound of that. To distract himself, he looked at the poem.

'What's it say?' his sister asked, looking over his shoulder.

He showed it to her. A baffling title stood over a piece of poetry just four mysterious lines long.

FastAg, changeable (11)

This beauty treatment makes you ugly
This medicine will cause your death
Think of a metal firm as water
The mirror shows your final breath

'What do you think it's about?' Miranda asked. 'It's kinda gruesome.' Although she was older than her brother, he was an avid reader of everything he could get his hands on, and she thought he had more chances of deciphering this message than she did.

'Don't know,' he said, accepting the unspoken assignment. 'I'll have to think.'

They looked at each other. Both knew that they were thinking the same thing. Miranda spoke it out loud: 'To Grandpa's study?'

'To Grandpa's study,' said her brother.

They started to run down the corridor to a room they had long thought of as their own personal Aladdin's Cave, filled with artefacts, books and fascinating objects, such as Oriental puzzle boxes, which they spent hours learning how to open.

But before they reached it, they heard a sound at the door. But this time, it was not a doorbell. Someone with a key was entering the house. Had their parents or their grandfather returned at last?

2

The Trouble Game

'We are going to be in massive trouble,' said the teacher, twirling the right side of his moustache, something he always did when he was nervous. Life had been stressful lately, which meant that the right side of his moustache was curly and came to a fine vertical point, just like a Victorian pantomime villain, while the left side drooped and ended in a blunt, slightly shaggy line.

His wife shook her head. 'It'll be fine. I've been very careful about this.'

The two teachers, Jay Aldred and Anya Modi, were the

only two teachers in school who knew that Mira and Marko Lee were living by themselves. They sat in the staff room, fretting.

Mr Aldred was convinced that they should have reported the children to the authorities. 'Not to get them in trouble—I know you wouldn't want that—but to make sure they are looked after. Anything could happen. Something horrible could happen. And then who will end up being blamed?'

Ms Modi gave him a tired half-smile. 'And that's your real concern, isn't it? That we'll end up in big trouble. Well, as I've told you before, I've been really careful. If they were younger, it would be illegal to leave them home alone, and I would definitely have reported them to the police. But Mira just scrapes into the "old enough" category.'

The male teacher spun the end of his moustache nervously. 'Look, we may be okay in legal terms, but that's not the point. We could still be criticised for not getting help for them.'

His wife knew that he was worried that they would lose their jobs. She shook her head. 'I don't think so. I visit them twice a week at least, they have a woman who comes for a few hours every other day to clean and cook, they're happy and healthy and their grades haven't particularly suffered. In most classes, they do okay, nothing special. They both got A's in History last week. They've become passionately interested in it. Look at this.'

She sorted through some papers and flipped two sheets over to her husband.

He scanned them and nodded. 'Wow,' he said. 'I see what you mean. They've gone from zeroes to heroes in the History department. What happened?'

Ms Modi leaned back in her chair and pondered for a while before answering.

'To be totally honest, I don't know. They've taken to hanging out in their grandfather's study. He was a very well-known historian and archaeologist. He's retired now. They spend hours reading his books and studying his artefacts.'

'You mean they are somehow teaching themselves? That doesn't make sense. I have a classroom full of books, but most of my students don't teach themselves anything. And you told me that the boy was a good reader but his sister was average.'

She nodded slowly. 'You're right. It's not just being surrounded by books. They have this really weird game they play. They sort of ...' her voice trailed off. She suddenly gave him a stern look.

'What?' he said, confused at the sudden hostility in her face.

'If I tell you, can you take off your super-sceptic hat for a moment? And don't make fun of me for half-believing what they tell me?'

'Me? Make fun of you? Would I ever do such a thing?'

'Yes,' she said. 'At least once a week.'

'Tell me,' he said, with a half-apologetic look.

She leaned forward and joined her hands together.

'Their grandfather found this thing called a magic mirror. It's an old artefact from China. You see them in museums sometimes. They sit around and look at their grandfather's books and pictures and collections, and then they play this game. They put the mirror into a small round window so that light shines right through it. It projects lines on the walls, making the room look different. Then they convince themselves that they are in a different time and place. So, for example, they, like 'found themselves' on Zheng He's treasure ship as it sailed the oceans, and on another occasion they 'went' to the Taklamakan desert with Marco Polo to meet the heirs of Genghis Khan. Only they don't think of it as a game. They see themselves as really time-travelling.'

He gave her an "aha" look. 'So that's how they've become so good at history. They study it, and then they act it out in games. That way it sticks in their minds. That's actually a brilliant way of learning. We should use it in other lessons.'

She didn't return his smile, but just looked thoughtful.

Now he was puzzled. 'What?'

She looked at him without replying.

He continued, 'Are you saying that they're *not* acting? That the mirror really is magic in some way? You don't believe in time travel, do you?'

She thought for another moment before shaking her head. 'No. Of course not. It *must* be some sort of imaginary game.' But she spoke with a curious lack of conviction.

'We ought to use their method in school more. Get the History classes to act out the periods of history they're studying,' her husband said.

She gave a single nod, still thoughtful.

'What is it?' he asked. 'There cannot be any other explanation, surely?'

'As you say, there can't be any other explanation. Yet at the same time, I find myself amazed at just how powerful the experience seems to be. When Mira first came to me and told me about Zheng He's ship, it was like she was talking about a real place, somewhere she'd spent several days exploring.'

'It just means she has a great imagination.'

'*Marko* is a book addict. I would expect him to have a great imagination. But Mira is not much of a reader. I can't work out where she gets all the details from. And ... there's something else, too.'

He had never seen her so puzzled. 'What?'

She pulled from her papers a sheet of paper showing a picture of an ancient metal disk, with scalloped edges. Chinese pictograms were finely etched on it. 'The magic mirror itself intrigues me, I mean, with my educator hat on.'

He looked at the picture. 'It looks a like a metal shield of some sort.'

She agreed. 'But it has a lot of strange qualities. First, you can polish it up and use it as a normal mirror, getting a reasonable sort of reflection. But if you hold it up to the light, so they say, the sun shines right through it. Or the moon, in the case of the kids' mirror.'

'It must be a very fine, thin metal.'

'So you'd think. But no. It's a fairly solid, thick metal. They're usually made of bronze. Scientists think it is made in such a way that there are tiny, invisible openings through which light flows. Maybe at a molecular level.'

'That's a bit weird.'

'That's not all that's strange. There are markings on it. So when a bright light shines through it, the markings are projected onto the walls.'

She paused for effect.

'And ...?' he prompted her.

'In several cases, scientists have found that the markings projected on the walls don't match the markings on the surface. It's a mystery.'

He sat back in his chair and knotted his fingers together. 'That does sound deliciously weird,' he said. 'I do love a touch of magic with my afternoon tea.'

They spent a few minutes in silence, with Jay Aldred looking at the papers on magic mirrors which his wife had collected.

When the bell went, she scooped up the papers and patted them into a neat stack. 'I've made up my mind,' she said. 'I'm going to go round to see Mira and her brother tonight. Or you can do it if I can't get out of visiting my grandma. We're not going to report them to the authorities, but I'm going to insist that they report themselves to some responsible guardians before the end of this week—not the police or the social workers, but family members. There must be an aunt, or a sister-in-law, or a family of cousins or someone who can take responsibility for them. Maybe just a neighbour.'

The other teacher agreed. 'Good idea. It's not right for you to take so much responsibility on your shoulders.'

They walked towards the door of the staff room.

'What have you got this afternoon?' he asked.

She wrinkled her nose to make an expression of distaste. 'Something pretty horrible,' she said. 'We're doing an art project supporting the Asian history module. It's basically looking at the first emperor of China. Brutality, madness, mass murder.'

'I have a departmental staff meeting. Pretty much the same.'

3

Puzzles and Polyester

As soon as the children had reached the door, Mrs Sun, the noisy neighbour, had flowed into the hall like a tsunami.

She had cooed over the youngsters and laid down several shopping bags at their feet. 'I've bought you some lovely surprises,' she said. 'You are going to LOVE these.'

'Er, thanks,' said Miranda, flashing a fake smile.

Mrs Sun fancied herself as a fashion designer, and had opened a boutique on a high street in town. Almost everything in the shop was designed by her—and almost everything was awful.

The large lady pulled out a luridly coloured bundle of polyester. 'Now this is for you, darling Miranda. It's perfect, don't you think?'

'Er, yeah, great. Did you design it yourself?'

'You can tell? Of course you can! A pretty young lady like you has an eye for what's happening in fashion.'

She bent over and felt around in the bags again. 'Now where is it? I have something for you too, young man. Ah, here it is.'

She pulled out a shirt in some sort of polyester print fabric. It was purple and orange.

'Eww,' said Marko.

'You like it? I knew you would,' gushed Mrs Sun. 'Now I want you two to put them on.'

'Right now?' Miranda asked.

Mrs Sun nodded. 'Of course. No time like the present.'

'But um ... um ...' Miranda wracked her brain to think of an escape plan. 'We have to go for a school activity right away. It's youth club tonight. We have to leave in like five minutes. So it's really kind of you to come, and we really love the gifts, but we kinda have to rush out. Almost immediately. In fact, we're already late.'

Mrs Sun's beaming smile got wider. 'That's perfect. You can launch the garments tonight. I want you to wear them to the youth club. I'm quite sure they'll get a lot of attention and then you can tell your friends where they can buy their own.'

She pointed to the doors that led off the hall. 'Now that can be the girls' changing room and that can be the boys' changing room. Chop-chop. I want to see you in them. And then I can drive you to the youth club. My driver is outside.'

Unable to escape, the two children picked up their new outfits and parted company to put them on. A few minutes later they entered the kitchen where Mrs Sun had gone to get herself a glass of water. The polyester garments were revolting.

'Beautiful,' she crooned. 'You will be the belles of the ball, so to speak. Now I'll just go to the toilet, and then I'll take you to school.'

As she disappeared, Marko turned to his sister. 'What do we do now? I'm NOT going out in these. And there's nothing at school tonight, is there? You just made that up.'

'I've got a plan,' she said. 'I'll write her a note saying that we decided to walk, because the youth club is meeting at a venue somewhere nearby. Then we can just go and hide somewhere. Pretend we're already out of the house.'

She scrawled a note as fast as she could while Marko listened carefully for the sound of approaching footsteps. Luckily, Mrs Sun was gone for several minutes.

Miranda placed the note on the woman's bag, and then the two of them raced off to hide under Grandpa's desk.

They waited in silence until they heard Mrs Sun leave. Then they returned to their mission.

***

Miranda's eyes widened as she sat in her grandfather's chair and re-read the letter. 'Yippee,' she said, turning to her brother. 'We're going to America. The town where Superman lives.'

'Superman? Show me,' said Marko, leaning over and scanning the letter. 'Where?'

She pointed to a particular line near the end of the handwritten text. 'There.'

'Two hundred and ten,' he read. 'Necropolis.' He glared at her and grabbed the letter. 'This doesn't say anything about Superman.'

'Don't you know anything?' she sneered. 'Necropolis is where Superman lives.'

He was silent for a moment, thinking. 'I don't think so,' he said eventually, his voice quiet. 'It's something like that, but not quite.' He tried to recall the name of the town, but it wouldn't come. 'I'll tell you what it is later,' he said.

Grandpa's letter was very simple. It read as follows:

Dear Miranda and Marko,

Thank you so much for arranging for your friend to deliver the map to me last month. It proved vital. I owe you much. Now the next stage of the mission is going to be difficult, for both of you, and for me. I want you to head to 210, the Necropolis. "There's something in there which I need you to get. It's a cubic puzzle which you need to retrieve."

On a separate sheet of paper I am giving you a puzzle poem. If you can work it out, it will help you learn a lot.

But one warning. In the place where you are going, there are lots of highly dangerous people. Please be very very careful.

You will bring the mirror of the moon with you of course. And you will take it back safely.

Your loving Ye-Ye

He signed off with the affectionate Chinese nickname for grandfather. The family was culturally mixed, with elements from both the east and the west.

'Okay,' said Miranda. 'It looks to me like the first thing we need to do is solve the puzzle of the poem.'

She spread it out on the table and stared at it. 'A second look should help,' she thought.

FastAg, changeable (11)

This beauty treatment makes you ugly

This medicine will cause your death

Think of a metal firm as water

The mirror shows your final breath

After a full minute of staring at it, the space between her eyebrows crinkled in annoyance. 'I don't know what it means. But it sounds really bad, whatever it means. Like it's talking about poison or something. It's something really evil, right? You think it is medicine, but it kills you. You think it's good for your beauty but it makes you ugly. What could it be?'

'I don't know. But metal which flows like water—that must be a reference to molten metal. You know how when you heat up metal and it goes white hot, it becomes like a liquid?'

'I guess. Maybe that's what it means. Molten metal. Do people put metal on their faces as a beauty treatment? If they did, what would happen? Wouldn't it burn their faces?'

Her brother nodded. 'It would. But I've never heard of anyone doing that. We're going to have to do more research.'

Miranda sat at the computer and looked up Wikipedia and Google. She found lots of information about molten metal, but nothing that seemed to match the clues in the poem.

Then she turned to her grandfather's physical encyclopaedia and looked up beauty products in it.

Marko took a different route. He looked up his grandfather's old books on history, looking for cultural clues.

After an hour had passed, they were getting frustrated. They had formed lots of vague ideas about what the poem could mean, but nothing which had actually clicked, nothing which looked like a solid clue that could unlock the meaning of the poem.

Most baffling—they decided—was the title: 'FastAg, changeable (11)'. What could that mean? When they looked it up on the Internet, they came up with lots of German companies. After another five minutes of research, they learned that AG was a German word meaning 'company', an abbreviation for Aktiengesellschaft.

Miranda blinked at the long, ugly word. 'I don't even want to try saying that,' she said. 'Do you think it means that Grandfather is in Germany?'

Marko pulled a face. 'I don't think so,' she said.

Another ten minutes of study proved equally fruitless. They decided to break for dinner. The housekeeper, Gwendy, had laid out some dishes for them, making sure they got a nutritious range of foods. When their parents had first disappeared the children had eaten huge amounts of ice cream and sugary foods, but they soon found themselves missing savoury foods, and even vegetables.

Then they had gradually got back to good dietary habits, eating a mixture of sweet items and savoury ones—although they still often ate dessert before the main course. There was a good reason for this. If you ate dessert first and then your main course, and you were still hungry, you could have a second dessert.

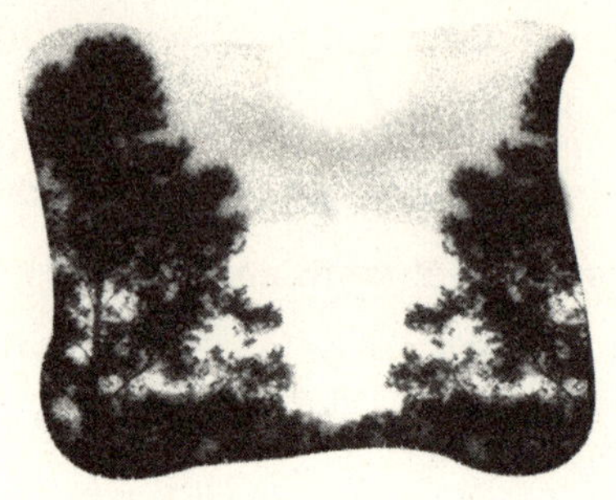

4

The Silver Moon

At 7:30 that night, the doorbell rang.

'You're closer,' said Mira.

'I got it earlier,' said Marko.

'I'm tired.'

'So am I.'

'It sounds like a boy. Probably for you.'

'It does not. What do you mean it sounds like a boy?' 'It smells like a boy.'

'You're making it up.'

'I'm not. Boys smell different from girls. It's a scientific fact. Look it up.'

Miranda looked sceptical. But then her curiosity got the better of her and she scampered out of the room and up the stairs to the remote viewer. She saw the top of an adult's head. She recognised Mr Aldred, husband of her favourite teacher.

A minute later she opened the door. 'Hello, Mr Aldred.'

'Good evening, Mira. Anya was going to come tonight but she got called away to visit her grandma. So she asked me to deliver this to you, and tell you that she wants to have dinner with you guys tomorrow, talk about some things.' He handed her a box of donuts.

'Wow, donuts, thanks! Do you want one?' she asked, pulling off the lid and offering him one of the six sparkling sugar-coated donuts.

'No thanks,' said the teacher. 'Oh go on then, I might have just one.' He pulled one out of the packet and ate it in two bites. 'I shouldn't,' he said, speaking with his mouth full. 'Anyway, she'll be over at seven-ish tomorrow night.' He turned to go.

But Marko came charging out of the room. 'Mr Aldred, can I ask you something? What does this mean?' He handed him a piece of paper. He read it carefully.

'It's a poem. Bit of an odd one, it seems to me.'

'The title. What does the title mean?'

He looked at it. 'FastAg, changeable (11).' After a few seconds, he smiled. 'That's easy,' he said. 'It's a cryptic crossword type clue. The answer is one word, eleven letters long, suggested by the words given. Give me another word for fast.' He looked at Marko.

'Speedy?'

'Quick?' said Miranda.

The teacher smiled at her. 'Write them down.' He pulled a pen out of his jacket pocket and wrote the words 'speedy' and 'quick' on the top of the donut box. 'Next, what does Ag stand for?'

'It means 'company' in German. We looked it up,' said Mira.

'True. But what ELSE could it mean?'

There was silence. 'What could it stand for?' he continued.

'Agriculture?' suggested the girl.

'True,' said the teacher. 'It could stand for Agriculture. But anything else? What do two-letter abbreviations often stand for? To chemists and scientists?'

'The periodic table,' said Miranda. She looked at her brother. 'You're good at that sort of thing. Is Ag an element?'

Marko nodded. 'It is. But I can't remember which one.'

'No more clues,' said Mr Aldred. 'The rest is up to you.'

The two children chewed their bottom lips as they thought. Marko decided to make a guess. 'I have a feeling it's gold or silver. Is that right?'

Mr Aldred wrote down the words 'gold' and 'silver' on the donut box. Now there were four words on the box: *speedy, quick, gold* and *silver*.

The two children stared at the four words, trying to make sense of them. 'Quicksilver,' Miranda said, slowly. 'That's a word, isn't it? I don't know what it means, though. Is it 11 letters?'

'It is!' said her brother, counting on his fingers.

'Okay, that's all I'm giving you. The rest you can work out yourself.'

The two children spent the next hour in front of the computer, mostly looking at Wikipedia pages. Within minutes of the teacher's departure they had learned that *quicksilver* was an old word for the chemical known as mercury—the liquidy silver stuff that you see in old-fashioned thermometers.

From then on, it was easy to work out the rest of the title from references in dictionaries and Wikipedia. They learned that there was a type of personality called 'mercurial' which meant 'changeable' and referred to people who changed their minds frequently and acted in an unpredictable way.

When they called up images of mercury, and saw the shining silver liquid, it was clear what the third line of the poem was referring to: 'metal flowing like water.' They also learned that mercury was the only metal that was a liquid at normal room temperature. Other metals had to be heated for them to become liquid.

The rest of the details in the poem gradually became clear as they read books from Grandpa's shelf, and files on the Internet. Romans and Egyptians thought mercury was good for the skin; sometimes they used it in cosmetics. In fact it was very bad for the skin: beauty treatments that make you ugly, and even kill you. They learned that the Mayan people used bowls of mercury as mirrors, not realising that the stuff could kill them—make them take their final breath.

And then they found the strangest story of all. Miranda found it first. It was the tale of an emperor who believed that mercury would help him live forever. He wanted rivers of mercury around his grave to bring him back to life. He ordered his men to build an underground 'city of the dead' for him to live in.

'What was his name?' Marko asked.

'I don't know how to pronounce it,' his sister replied. 'Qin Shi Huang. Something like that.'

Marko grabbed one of Grandpa's old books and started flicking through the pages at high speed. 'I read about him. I know the story. We did it in school. He was a bad man. Really, really bad. Wait. Let me find it.'

It took him a minute, but he found the story in an old book of Chinese history.

He was the first Emperor of China, and he spent three days with Anqi Sheng, a one-thousand-year-old magician who was planning to live forever. The Emperor became convinced that he too could live forever, and he looked for ways to make himself immortal.

'What's that?' Marko said suddenly, looking up.

'What's what?' his sister asked. But by that time, she had heard it too.

Someone had entered through the front door.

'Mrs Sun is back,' whispered Marko. 'She must have seen the lights on.'

Footsteps approached the door.

***

Miranda opened the wooden box on Grandpa's desk and pulled out the magic mirror, a disk of metal with a slightly greenish hue. 'We need to escape,' she said, biting her lip.

She found the mirror enchanting, but also scary—she had definitely seen a green-eyed face in its cloudy surface that was not her own.

Marko grabbed his red school backpack, which would hold the mirror when they weren't using it—and which acted as a bit of a security blanket for him.

The moon had started to shine brightly. Miranda, who was much taller than her brother, held the disk up to the small round window.

The room was bathed in light.

'Where are we going?' Marko asked.

'To number 210, the Necropolis,' his sister said. 'Wherever that is.'

The light grew unnaturally bright until they could see nothing. They closed their eyes against the glare.

Then suddenly everything went black. The floor seemed to fall out from under them, and they started falling too.

5

The Chamber

They landed. The sense of movement and disorientation disappeared. Gravity returned. But the darkness remained. Miranda felt a change in the texture of the ground beneath her feet. Gone was the old rug in Grandpa's office. Now there was an earthen texture—a firm but yielding and uneven surface. She spoke urgently to her brother. 'I can't see anything.'

'Me neither. We must have arrived at night.'

'We left at night.'

'Yeah, but we must have arrived at some place before they invented lights. It's too dark. No lampposts, no stars even.'

Something in the quality of the sound their voices made led her to realise they were indoors. She spoke in a low whisper, 'We're inside a house with no windows. I don't think we should be talking.'

'Why not?'

'Because we don't know who else is in here. We could be in a room full of people. Remember Grandpa said there were dangerous people around here? What if we are in the middle of the bad guy's sleeping chamber or something?'

'I don't think so. We'd be able to hear him snore.'

'Not everybody snores.'

'Bad guys do.'

'How do you know?'

'I just do. That's the sort of thing bad guys do. Bad guys snore, good guys don't snore. Can you imagine Batman snoring? No way.'

'You're talking *rubbish*. As usual. You read too much.' She paused to think. 'Anyway, there's no one here. I can't hear anyone breathing or moving or anything. Wherever we are, it's deserted.'

'Wait. I've got a light.'

He put the mirror into his red school backpack and pulled out a small flashlight and turned it on. They were in a windowless room, with earthen walls and floors. Perhaps a cave. There were mats on the floor, with goblets nearby. It seemed to be a rest chamber of some sort. There was an opening at one end, closed off with a makeshift curtain. Miranda poked her head through the gap. Then quickly gestured to her brother to turn off the flashlight.

'What is it? What did you see?'

'There are huge guards outside.'

'Are we prisoners?'

'I think so.'

'That's terrible,' the boy said. 'How do we escape? We've only just got here and we've been caught. No, wait. We can't be prisoners. The doors aren't locked.'

'It's a curtain. You can't lock curtains.'

'That's what I mean. If we were prisoners, the doors would be wooden or metal or something. They're just curtains. I think this is someone's room. Someone important.'

'That would explain the silver goblets.'

In the darkness, they gently moved to the mats and found the silver goblets. Marko sniffed one. 'It's water,' he said.

'How do you know?'

'I smelled it.'

'Water doesn't have a smell.'

'Yes, it does.'

'What does it smell of?'

'It smells watery.'

'Shut up.'

'You shut up.'

'It's cold water. I am going to drink mine.'

'You talk such rubbish all the time. You can smell boys. You can smell water. Where do you get these ideas?'

'I can smell adults,' he said suddenly, cocking his head to one side.

Sure enough there was the unmistakable scent of men moving—sweat, leather, metal. This was accompanied by the sound of men's voices and other sounds indicating movement—the clanking sound of equipment being moved.

Miranda and Marko raced to the curtain. There were men entering the cave-like corridor, but some distance away. The two children raced into the corridor and ran in the opposite direction, away from the activity.

'We're in the past, aren't we?' Miranda said. 'I can tell by how the people are dressed. The ground is muddy but no one's got Wellington boots or anything like that. What year do you think it is?'

'Don't know. But we're probably at a time when mercury was really important. Maybe in the time of the first Emperor of China? That would make sense, wouldn't it? He liked mercury and wanted to build an underground city. Mira, stop walking so fast. I think we should stop.'

The corridor they had chosen became increasingly dark. Marko wanted to turn back. But Miranda kept moving forward.

'Stop,' he said. 'Come back.'

But she hurried steadily forward.

He thought about stopping and turning back. But then he realised that he would be left alone in the dark in this mysterious underground warren. And that would be even scarier than heading forward, after his sister. So he scampered ahead to catch up with her.

'It'll be pitch-dark if we go any further,' he said.

'No,' Mira said. 'There's a light ahead. Way ahead.'

Suddenly there were sounds behind them—voices again. She started running faster, spooked by the dark and the sounds behind them. She intended to get to the doorway of the lit room and then stop to peek in. But as she came to a halt, all forty kilos of a small boy slammed into her from behind.

The two of them tumbled into a large chamber carved into the tunnel. In it were a group of powerful-looking men sitting around a table.

The biggest, scariest looking one turned to face them. 'Well, what do we have here?' he asked. The men looked hostile, angry to have been interrupted. One man reached for his sword handle. Another picked up an axe.

Miranda, terrified, gave a smile and waved her hand. 'Hi,' she said with fake cheeriness. 'How you guys doing? Nice cave.'

***

The men stared at the two children. But the initial looks of hostility changed to expressions of intense curiosity.

Miranda was puzzled. Did they not have children in this community? Then she realised that they were looking at their clothes.

'Who are you?' said a tall man with a small, pointed beard and thick eyebrows. He was elegantly dressed in a blue robe, which appeared highly unsuitable for mining, or whatever similar activity was taking place here.

'We are, we are ...' stammered Miranda. Then she had an idea. 'We are the children of the Emperor,' she barked. That was probably the best line to make sure they were not immediately put to death. Then a thought struck her. What if this group of people hiding furtively underground were rebels, plotting to kill the Emperor? Had she said the worst possible thing?

The man with the pointed beard looked at them, his eyes narrowing, suspicion in them. 'Welcome,' he said, carefully. 'What are your names?'

Miranda was struck dumb. She had no idea what the Emperor's children had been called. She tried to think back to what she had read. The children had been boys, hadn't they? Was one called Fugu or something like that? Or was that a type of fish?

Marko raised his hand. The movement caught Miranda's eye. 'You don't have to put your hand up to talk,' she whispered. 'This isn't school.'

The man turned his gaze to him.

'We are the youngest children,' Marko said. 'We are 27 and 28.'

There was a chuckle. The large man nodded. 'That sounds like the Emperor. So many wives and concubines with such large broods that he gives them numbers instead of names. Typical.'

The other men murmured their assent.

The man with the beard, who looked to be the leader, stepped closer to them. 'I am Zhao Gao,' he said. 'You were sent to find me?'

'Er, yes,' said Miranda. 'The Emperor, I mean, our father, wanted you to look after us, give us food and drink, make sure we were all right, had a place to sleep and so on.'

'He sent you without servants?'

'They dropped us off. They had to go on. He had other jobs for them to do.'

The man looked down at their clothes again. 'Your garments are very fine. Is this silk? A new type?' His fingers felt the sleeve of her polyester top.

She nodded. 'Yeah. It's a new type of silk called, er, polyester. Very rare. Only children of the Emperor are allowed to have it.'

He turned his eyes on Marko's shirt. He focused on a glint of metal at the boy's waistline—the buckle of a belt. Then he noticed the metal rivets in the boy's jeans.

Zhao said: 'And you have metal embedded in your clothing. That is very fine.'

Marko looked down at the studs in the corners of the various seams in his jeans. 'You want to see something amazing? Look at this. It's a new invention. It's called a zip.'

He lowered the zip of his jeans a couple of centimeters and then pulled it up again.

'That's disgusting!' said Miranda. 'Stop it. You can be arrested for that.'

But Marko's action had had the desired effect. Zhao looked stunned.

A man behind him sprang forward and gazed at the boy's zipper. The man breathed: 'Metal which is pliable, as soft as cloth, and which opens and closes at will.'

The boy was wise enough to ram home the advantage he had won for them. 'ONLY the Emperor's children get this sort of thing,' said Marko. 'It was invented especially for us. We call this part of the garment a fly.'

'Why?' asked the man.

The boy's brow wrinkled. 'I don't know.' He turned to his sister. 'You know, I never thought about that. Why are they called flies? They don't fly.'

The atmosphere in the room changed. Now all the weapons had been lowered and the men were standing in some reverence.

'Thank you, Levi-Strauss,' Miranda mumbled.

Zhao Gao bowed slightly. 'Welcome to the Necropolis,' he said.

6

City of the Dead

When Zhao Gao offered to organise a tour for them, the children were not enthusiastic. Who wants to spend hours trekking through dark underground tunnels?

But then they realised that this would be the best way to learn about where they were—and to find room 210. So, after a quick consultation between themselves, they happily accepted the offer, and were delighted to find that much of the tour was on the surface.

The first thing the Emperor's representative did was to

take them up to ground level. It was not night in this place, but late afternoon.

What they saw stunned them. They were in a huge building site, which seemed to stretch from horizon to horizon. Zhao explained, 'Necropolis means "city of the dead", as I am sure you know. As you can see, this really is a city.'

They stood at one end of a rather flat plain and they saw activity as far as their eyes could see. In the centre of the scene there was a large cluster of individuals working, not just hundreds but thousands of men. And literally scores of tents for housing them. To the far right, there were more men and buildings, and some kind of mine was being dug. To their left there was a long trail of carts carrying huge amounts of what looked like red soil. The trail stretched into the far distance.

'What are all these people doing?' Miranda asked.

Zhao said, 'What aren't they doing? That would be a better question. They are doing everything you would expect in an operation where a city was being built. They are digging, they are building, they are making roads, they are planting trees, they are carving statues, they are designing and carving and cutting and shaping all manner of materials.'

He pointed to the right cluster. 'There will be houses and temples here, while over there is a huge, manufacturing operation. We are creating the biggest, toughest army the world has ever known.'

Then he pointed to the central cluster. 'In the centre, and at various positions towards the perimeter, there will be huge underground works, a series of chambers, some extremely large, many with special purposes. They will stretch all the way to the chamber from which we have just emerged.'

Marko pointed to the long line of carts bearing a reddish powder. 'Is that soil?' he asked. 'Why are they bringing in so much extra earth? If they need soil for something, can't they just use the stuff the tunnel builders dig up?'

Zhao nodded. 'We will use the stuff that the tunnel builders dig up for sure,' he said. 'But we need more—much much more.'

'Why?' the boy asked. 'What will you do with it?'

'We're going to build a mountain,' he said. 'Normally the gods build mountains. But your father has decided that he would like his own mountain, so I told him that he can have one.' 'How can people build a mountain? That's impossible, surely?'

Zhao started walking, and the two children followed. 'I would say that building your own mountain is *almost* impossible. Or to put it another way, it has been impossible up to now. But I am good at doing the impossible. Your father, as you surely know, has a habit of asking for the impossible. And I am good at delivering—which of course is how I reached the exalted position at which I stand.'

He walked faster, towards an old brown tent.

'There are two things you need to build your own mountain, I discovered,' he continued. 'The first is inexhaustible resources, in terms of human labour, money and determination. The second is an architect who won't say no to anything. And here he is. General Meng.'

He pointed inside the tent. They saw a large man with a white beard. He stood with a group of other men looking at plans on a paper on a large table.

'Zhao,' the chief architect said, looking up.

'I bring visitors,' replied Zhao, gesturing at the children with a slight movement of his head. 'Two of the Emperor's children.'

General Meng nodded, but did not smile. He looked wary. There seemed to be no love for the Emperor—respect, maybe, or fear, but no love.

Zhao said, 'Can you get one of your people to show them around?'

Meng nodded. 'What are their names?'

'Twenty-seven and twenty-eight,' Zhao said.

Meng gave a brief laugh that sounded more like a bark. 'That makes sense.' He turned to the children. 'Your father likes to make things easy for himself, doesn't he? Rewrites the rules all the time, rules of the law books, rules of physics, rules of the gods. Anything to make his own life better. Well, our job is not to ask questions. We do what he requests.'

He turned and talked quietly to a woman standing nearby. 'Take them to camp 14 and find someone who will give them something to do.'

The two children followed the woman out of a back tent flap, leaving Zhao and Meng talking.

As they walked in the dust behind her, Miranda realised that their position was somewhat precarious. What if the Emperor's *real* children turned up? What if they said or did something that showed that they had no relationship with the ruler? Punishment would probably mean death.

'What shall we do?' she whispered to her brother. 'Do you think we should try to escape?'

He shook his head. 'No, I think we need to get a detailed tour. That's the only way we'll find out where to get what Grandpa wants and deliver it where he needs it to go.'

'But what if they find out we are not really the Emperor's children?'

'We're miles away from the palace in which he hangs out.

I read that in Grandpa's book. The capital city is several days' travel away from the Necropolis.'

Miranda said, 'We need to find room 210.'

Her brother shook his head. 'No,' he said. 'That's not an address. That's the date. I remember it from school now. This is 210 BC.'

They walked in silence for a while, taking in that remarkable thought.

Marko said, 'So the king isn't likely to pop over to the building site to visit. This is long before there was any sort of transport except carts and things. We should be safe.'

'Thank goodness for polyester,' said Miranda. 'They'd never seen it before. I can't believe they think it's cool. God bless Mrs Sun.'

The woman took them towards a tent so large that it seemed to be as long as an airport building.

'Wow,' said Marko. 'I've never seen a tent so large. Look, it must have chimney openings, too.' He pointed to an area on the left where smoke was pouring neatly upwards.

They entered the tent and stopped dead in their tracks.

In the gloom, a large battalion of dangerous-looking soldiers stood at attention, staring right at them. Arrows glinted. Crossbows were poised. Razor-sharp spears were grasped, ready to be thrust.

7

Immortal Guardians

It had been a busy evening. They had spent the last hour with an old man named Tang and his daughter Hsiao Ta. Tang was one of the master craftsmen for the project.

Camp 14 appeared to be the final assembly point of a line of factory-produced clay people. There was a whole battalion of armed men holding weapons.

'My job is the people,' Tang had explained. 'A necropolis is a city and a city needs people, right? So my job is to build the people.'

Mira asked, 'But how can you build a whole city full of people. Isn't that impossible?'

He shook his head. 'It should be impossible. But most things which are said to be impossible are actually just very difficult. There's not much difference between 'impossible' and 'extremely tough'. The people who realise this are the ones who agree to do impossible things, and somehow achieve them. Your father is the Emperor of the impossible. It seems he asks only for impossible things, and somehow, we have to deliver what he wants.'

Again, Miranda heard the fear in the speaker's voice. The Emperor was a dangerous man.

Craftsman Tang pointed to the ranks of soldiers. 'This is the final assembly area. We have different departments with various specialities. Some make only legs, some make arms, some make torsos, some make heads. Then within each group, we have specialities too. The leg people make straight legs or kneeling legs or sitting legs. The head people—they make a range of different head shapes, with different faces, different hats, different beards.'

The two children were amazed. 'And then you stick all the bits together?'

The old man nodded. 'We do. The parts are hollow, so they are not too heavy to lift. But each section has to be carefully assembled, and then the clay melted just enough that the parts bond together without breaking. It's a difficult job.'

'And then when they're finished they come here,' said Hsaio Ta. 'This is the best part.'

Tang smiled at his daughter. 'I guess she's right, this is the best bit. In all the other parts of the operation, we are just handling lumps of clay, and moulds, and doing fairly basic carving operations. But here we have the people-finishing department.'

'I finished one myself last week,' said the girl. She did not look much older than Mira, but had a certain self-assuredness that gave her an adult air.

Mira realised that at this time in history, people probably left school quite young, especially if they belonged to the working classes rather than the nobility. And girls probably had little education if any. Perhaps Hsiao Ta was thirteen or fourteen, but had probably been working for four or five years already.

Her father smiled at her. 'She did a great job. We work on their faces, turning them into individuals. Then we paint them in realistic colours. That's a long and difficult job, taking hours for each person. Finally, they are left to dry.'

'My one's a girl soldier dressed as a boy,' said the girl.

Miranda smiled. 'Let me guess,' she said. 'Is her name Fa Mulan?'

'No, it's Xiao Liu,' Hsaio Ta said.

Marko said to Miranda: 'The story of Fa Mulan is hundreds of years old, but we're two thousand years in the past.'

She turned to him. 'How do you know this stuff?'

He shrugged. 'I read,' he said. The boy jumped to his feet and walked up to one of the soldiers. 'The weapons seem real,' he said, peering at the blade of a spear.

'They are real,' said Tang. 'Every single one of them. Don't touch the blades. They are very sharp. That's one of the things that makes this army so valuable.'

Mira asked: 'How come the weapons are real but the people aren't?'

Tang wrinkled his brow. 'I guess you haven't had as much education as you should have. You probably learn different things at the schoolhouse in the Emperor's palace. But even Hsiao Ta can answer that question.'

'Don't you know how it works?' the girl asked. 'Life after death? When you make a model of something and dedicate it to the afterlife—you have to do a special ceremony—then it becomes real in the afterlife.'

Tang continued the explanation. 'Having to serve the Emperor in this area, we've all become experts in the subject of immortality. Representations come to life. If it is a dead statue it will become a live human being. If it is a corpse of a live human being, it will be reanimated. If it's a small scale model of something, it will grow to the proper size. So our great leader will have his thriving city.'

Marko put up his hand to ask a question. 'Please sir, is the city going to have only soldiers? Won't it be a bit boring if there are no other kinds of people?'

Tang smiled. 'Come for a walk,' he said. 'I'll show you some of the special things we are making for your father.'

Tang and his daughter took them on a tour of some of the other tents. There were people making entertainers in the first tent. Miranda particularly liked a life-sized clay model of a man who had a faraway look in his eyes and was holding up one hand with a finger pointed.

'That's a storyteller,' Hsiao Ta said. 'Very important in the afterlife.'

There were also acrobats and jugglers. In another tent, they saw chariots, more than a hundred. Three in particular were spectacular. 'The Emperor will ride around the Necropolis doing his inspections in these chariots,' Hsiao Ta said. 'The front one, his escort, is smaller, with room for only one driver, covered with a bronze umbrella. The second one is behind, much larger, pulling a carriage with windows in front and on the sides, and a door behind. A large circular umbrella keeps the rain and the sun off the Emperor's head. Many of the fittings are made of cast gold and silver and are very valuable.'

Then there was a chariot which looked like a firebird, black in front, red at the back. Six clay horses pulled the fearsome dark machine. The wheeled cart had wings bristling with rockets and a tail of tubes filled with arrows. 'This is the Phoenix chariot. It launches flaming rockets from its tail,' Tang said. 'Would you like to ride on it?'

'Is it dangerous?' Marko asked.

'Come and see,' the man replied.

'It really looks like a bird,' Marko said, gazing at the metallic feathers as he climbed on board.

'Of course,' said the girl. 'It's supposed to be a firebird.'

'And the tail moves like a machine gun,' said Marko, making rat-tat-tat-tat-tat noises as he turned the tail gun on imaginary enemies.

In the chariot in the next tent, Miranda sat in the driver's seat under a round metal umbrella. Hsiao Ta stood at the front of the chariot and pretended to wave a long spear.

Craftsman Tang laughed at the children. 'I'm tired of war,' he said, with a sigh. 'I dream of the day when these things can be magically transformed into children's toys displaying fireworks instead of machines for war.'

'Everything is built for fighting and killing,' Miranda said. 'Doesn't Dad ask you to make anything peaceful?'

Tang looked at the leader of the chariot-making staff silently for a moment before answering. 'The Emperor is a great man, there is no doubt about that. Eleven years ago, he sent the generals to secure peace for our frontiers. It was the first time that people everywhere, All Under Heaven, were united under one leader. And we hoped that the new law and order would bring harmony.'

A soldier standing with the chariot-makers shook his head. 'But since I've returned from the frontier, I've seen fear and hardship ruling the people instead.'

'Yes,' Craftsman Tang nodded. 'The Emperor you left is not the same one you've come back to serve.'

***

The rest of the tour was breathtaking.

There was an area called the chamber of entertainers containing acrobats. The storyteller she had seen earlier was due to be assigned to this room too, Hsiao Ta explained.

There was also an entire underground district called the Water Realm, a system of rivers where the Emperor could hunt, fish, or just enjoy sitting by the brook. The water system had bronze cranes standing in real water.

When they got back to the main tent, they were bedazzled by all they had seen.

'What about the fish in the water realm?' Marko asked. 'Will they be real?'

'We'll use real fish,' said Tang. 'I can make statues of seabirds, waders and so on. But I have not yet worked out how to make a clay or bronze fish that really swims. So we'll stock the ponds with live carp.' He opened his mouth to speak again, but a trumpet sounded. And then another one.

Everybody froze. They heard running feet.

A breathless soldier appeared at the door of the tent.

'He's here,' he gasped. 'All are to gather on the Western plain to greet him.'

Miranda's mouth dropped open. 'Uh-oh,' she said out of the side of her mouth to her brother. 'We are dead meat.'

8

Death and Sorcery

The two children gazed around, looking for a hole into which they could disappear. But everyone was moving in one direction, towards the main door of the tent.

Old Tang the master craftsman grabbed hold of them. 'You must come too, of course. We will find a place for you in front.'

'No, I'm feeling rather tired,' said Miranda. 'I think I want to go and lie down. Can you just show me to my tent? Is there like a presidential suite for the royal family?'

The old man just laughed as if she had made a good joke, and continued to gently usher the two youngsters along the stream of people heading out of the tent and towards a big river of people.

'I forgot my bag,' Miranda said desperately.

'You had no bag,' the man replied.

'I mean, my brother's bag.'

'He's wearing his bag on his back. Ingenious design,' said Craftsman Tang. 'I must study it and create one for myself.'

There seemed to be no escape.

Luckily, the crowds grew thicker and thicker as they moved ahead. She realised that it would be only a matter of time before the crush of bodies was so thick that she and Marko could easily slip away unnoticed.

She grabbed her brother's hand. 'We better not lose each other,' she hissed. 'As soon as we can, we slip away and go hide somewhere. We do NOT want to meet "our dad".'

Within a minute, they found an opportunity to part from Tang and his daughter. They weaved and ducked through the crowds like salmon swimming upriver, and eventually broke away from the river of people, running into a gap between two large ornate tents.

They turned a corner and ran straight into Zhao Gao and his men, who looked at them curiously. 'You are going the wrong way, young masters,' he said. 'Everyone else is going to the western plain.'

'I forgot something,' lied Miranda unconvincingly.

Zhao looked at her suspiciously. He grabbed her upper arm firmly. 'I think you should come with us,' he said. 'I want to make sure you two get good seats. So you can see him and he can see you.'

They marched the two children back towards the plain.

Five minutes later, they reached a large field where a huge number of people—must have been tens of thousands—were seated on the floor before a large stage. The children were delivered into the hands of Craftsman Tang and his daughter once again.

All attention was focused on a small group of men on a raised plinth made of wood. One in particular caught everyone's attention. He was dressed in white robes and had a curious white hat on his head. His hands were lost in large, wide sleeves. He had a long beard and his eyes were nested in wrinkles.

'Is that the Emperor, I mean, my dad?' Marko asked Hsiao Ta. 'I mean, I know what my dad looks like, of course, being his son, but er, I can't see very well from here. I don't have my long range glasses on.'

'You are strange,' Hsiao Ta said, looking at him in puzzlement. 'Always making odd jokes. Jokes which are not funny, just strange. Are you really telling me you don't know who that is?'

'The guy with the beard? Ah ...'

The girl laughed. 'I can't tell whether you are joking or not.' Then her eyes grew bright. 'That is the sorcerer.'

'The sorcerer?'

'Xufu the Sorcerer. The Emperor's personal alchemist. I have never seen a sorcerer before, let alone the greatest in the world. Have you?'

Miranda, who had been listening to the conversation, turned to the stage and stared.

***

'Is he going to do magic tricks?' Marko asked.

'Don't be silly,' Miranda snapped. 'He's not that kind of sorcerer.'

But Hsiao Ta put her head to one side. 'Well, sometimes he does, so they say. He can do magic if he wants. But that's not the main reason he's here.'

'Why is he here?' asked Miranda.

In reply, Hsiao Ta started looking around for her father. 'My father will tell you better than I.' She turned to him. 'The Emperor's children want to know why the sorcerer is here.'

Tang gave them an indulgent look and shook his head. 'The most expensively educated children in the whole world probably, and you know so little. Why am I not surprised?' He sighed, and then his voice took on a storytelling tone.

'You know your father is obsessed with the idea of living forever. He has made many attempts to solve the problem of death. Ten years ago, he ordered the court alchemists to create a potion that would make him live forever. Numerous potions were created. They gave concentrated doses to slaves, to test them out. In every case, the slave fell severely ill or died. The alchemists were punished. They were put to death.'

Marko gulped. 'Our father is a ... er ... harsh man.'

'Very harsh. In cases where he got angry he gave the alchemists to his lieutenants, Li Si and Zhao Gao, whom you have met. They are experts in slow, painful deaths. Li Si, the Supreme Minister of Justice, is known as the Chancellor of Fear, the Prince of Pain, the Master of Slow Death.'

'But if our dad kills anyone who fails, surely no one will want to even try?'

Tang looked thoughtful for a moment. 'When the Emperor wants something, he gets it. He ordered that all books of science and magic in the kingdom be burned. Thousands of volumes of wisdom disappeared in a few weeks. More than 460 alchemists were put to death in the following days. The result is that the remaining ones have only one subject to study: immortality for the Emperor. Their minds are focused tightly, shall we say? What's more, the incentive to find the answer is great. Failure to do so leads to the opposite of immortality. Death.'

Marko raised his hand. 'Did this sorcerer guy find immortality? Is that why he wasn't killed along with the others?'

Tang looked down at the small boy. 'Correct,' he said. 'To some extent. Xufu found the *address* of immortality. He found a location where the elixir of life is hidden. He found it two years ago.'

'So why didn't he bring it back for the Emperor, I mean, our Dad?'

'He tried. He went on a great expedition through the Bohai Sea and the Yellow Sea. He got close to it, or so he said, but had to turn back. He returned to the Emperor, made a report, and requested extra resources. Now he is returning to the quest—this time, with a much bigger fleet, determined to get it and bring it back.'

The last words of his story had to be shouted because the trumpets had started playing, and cheers went up from the crowds of workers.

Miranda heard a strange crunching sound, almost a rumble, but with a rhythm to it, something like the beating of a drum. She and thousands of other people turned their heads to the east to figure out where it was coming from. Clouds of dust rose from the plain.

9

Mount of the Gods

An army appeared to be approaching. Except it appeared to be an army of very short people—and none of the members had helmets or spears or shields. As they approached, Miranda's mouth dropped open. It was an army of children.

There were literally thousands of young people, from about her age—she guessed—to about eighteen or nineteen years old—a platoon of teenagers.

A horn sounded from the stage, and people's eyes were drawn back to the sorcerer. He moved towards a mounted tube, thin and opening into a cone shape—a primitive megaphone of some sort. And he began to speak.

'I am Xu Fu, Court Sorcerer of the Emperor of Qin,' he said.

There were loud cheers. Clearly this man was respected and loved. The roar continued for several minutes, and did not stop until the sorcerer raised his hands to call for silence.

Then he continued, 'I bring you exciting news of our mission—the mission you and I share, to bring immortality to our great leader. You are creating the Necropolis for the moment when he will transcend his earthly human body and become immortal. I am travelling to the Mount of the Gods, Pengli, to get the elixir of life which will make him immortal.'

This was followed by more cheering from the huge crowd.

The sorcerer said he had to speak about his mission. 'It is a long and complex story, and I must start at the beginning,' he said.

He reported that many years ago, the Emperor had spent three days with Anqi Sheng, a magician who had just reached his one-thousandth birthday.

'You might find that hard to believe, but the old magician gave many indisputable signs that he was more than a thousand years old. He knew things that even our wisest people had forgotten. He could forecast the future. He had a tiny vase which contained the light of the sun.'

Miranda turned to her brother. 'A flashlight?' she asked.

The sorcerer continued, 'He had a tiny silver box of fire.'

'A lighter,' her brother breathed.

'He performed many signs and wonders before disappearing magically.'

'It's Grandpa, it's got to be.'

Marko nodded, too excited to speak.

'But Anqi Sheng left behind one object. A cube with a message,' the sorcerer continued. 'This object has been placed in the royal chamber of the Necropolis and sealed there. The message said it represents earthly chains. One day it will simply vanish. And so will the bonds that tie the Emperor to this mortal life.'

Xu Fu went on to explain that Qin Shi Huang had asked him to track down Anqi Sheng to get more information. 'He told me to go to Mount Penglai, the abode of the gods.'

'Cool,' said Marko.

'Do you know about this?' Hsiao Ta asked.

'I think so,' the boy replied. 'I read about it in a book. It's an island, isn't it?'

The girl nodded. 'Yes. It's where the immortals gather once a year to eat their annual feast.'

They lapsed into silence and listened as the sorcerer described his visit to the waters around Mount Penglai. He explained that he had not been able to land on the island, but had seen it from a distance. 'The sands of the island are white, the grass is white, and the trees have white leaves. But the berries are made of rubies and diamonds. Gold and platinum palaces line the sides of the mountain. On the peak is a great golden palace where the immortals meet with Anqi Sheng.'

Xu Fu told the audience that they had set sail from the Bay of Bohai on the coast in the summer, two years earlier. They had rejoiced to see Mount Penglai in the distance. But they found their path blocked by a great sea monster and by powerful magic. Rather than let the mission fail, Xu Fu had returned home to build a greater army so that he could go back and fulfill the mission.

'Three moons ago, a crew of sailors returned from the task the Emperor had set them: to kill the great sea beast in the waters of Bohai between us and the island of Mount Penglai. That cleared the path for the launching of the great second mission, the mission to find and bring home the elixir of life. And that great mission is launched today,' he said.

The crowd roared at the top of their voices.

After letting the shouting continue for some time, the

sorcerer explained that the new fleet consisted of 60 barques crewed by 5000 of the finest sailors in the kingdom. There was also a troop of 3000 young people—the junior army that stood to one side of the stage. 'Their purity will overcome the barriers of dark magic that prevent mortals from landing on the island,' the magician continued.

The army of youngsters waved their hands and received cheers in return.

Miranda cheered too, but Marko touched her hand.

'I think I read something about this in Grandpa's history books,' he whispered to her. 'There were rumours about why he should need three thousand young people. They called it the fleet of virgins. Some people said the sailors planned to sacrifice them to get the gods on their side.'

'Eww,' said Miranda. 'That is mean.'

Sorcerer Xufu stepped back from his position at the centre of the stage and there was a period of chanting, followed by various ceremonies involving dancers with scrolls and beast-heads. And then the meeting was over.

'Did you hear what he said?' Miranda whispered to her brother. 'The thing that Anqi Sheng left is in the Necropolis, in the royal chamber. That's where we need to go. That's what Grandpa wants us to get. I think it was stolen from him and we have to get it back.'

He shook his head. 'No,' he said. 'The sorcerer said that when the cube vanishes, it will be a sign. I think that's our job. To make it vanish.'

As the crowd began to disperse, Mira turned to Hsiao Ta. 'Can we see the royal room in the Necropolis?' Miranda asked. 'It wasn't in our tour.'

The girl shook her head. 'Of course not,' she said. 'It is closely guarded. No one can go in.'

'Is it, like, totally impossible? I mean, could someone sneak in without getting permission?'

'If anyone went in, they would never get out again,' said Hsiao Ta. 'The guards would make sure of that.'

Miranda bit her lip and thought about that for a while. 'Could the guards be bribed or something?'

The girl shook her head. 'The royal death chamber is guarded by the ghost brigade,' she said. 'Those guards are already dead. There's nothing they want or need.'

Marko felt suddenly chilled. He gulped before asking, 'When you say they are already dead, do you mean they are statues?'

She shook her head gravely. 'No. They are ghosts. Heavily armed ghosts. Last month a builder accidentally went too near the royal death chamber. A ghost shot him dead with a crossbow bolt. No one can go anywhere near it.'

Miranda sighed. She thought of her grandfather's letter. This definitely was turning out to be a difficult mission. She needed to consult an expert. She sneaked into the dark of the nearest tunnel entrance.

***

Miranda stood in the dark with the magic mirror, which she had pulled out of her brother's backpack when he had gone to a well with Hsiao Ta to get some water.

'Are you there? Guardian, are you there?'

The first time they had used the mirror, she thought she saw the reflection of her own face in the cloudy mirror, but the eyes had blinked at a time when she was sure her own eyes had not moved. Then, several weeks later, she had woken up in the night and seen a face in the mirror—a beautiful but dangerous face, a green-tinged image. The person, or creature, had called itself the Guardian, and shown her some hourglasses. Each represented a life, and the Guardian had warned her that every decision she made, every action she took, either added to or subtracted from the number of grains of sand in the top of the glass. Each grain represented a possible future, and if she put herself in danger, the number of grains would diminish dramatically.

In the cold light of morning, the whole experience had seemed absurd; it must have been a dream or something.

But perhaps not; it had all seemed so real. And the information that the Guardian had given her had definitely helped them.

And now that they were in a difficult situation, it seemed vital to get all the help they could. 'Guardian, are you there? Can you hear me?'

The mirror glowed green and eyes blinked open through a grey-green fog.

'What do we do? I don't think we can get to the cube thing. It's pretty well protected. There's like this army of ghosts around it, they tell us.'

The thing in the mirror did not react.

Miranda continued: 'Can you give us any advice?'

Silence.

'Please,' she added, remembering her manners.

The silence continued. The eyes blinked, but the lips did not move.

'Well, I'm putting you back in the bag then, if you're not going to be of any help. Your choice.'

The lips parted and a whispering voice spoke. 'The time is up. This is the final day. What you have to do, you have to do now,' it said.

Then the image faded and she looked at a dull sheet of patterned bronze again.

'Gee, thanks,' said Miranda. 'That was really helpful.'

Suddenly she heard a sound behind her. She turned to see Hsiao Ta standing in the shadows, Marko behind her.

'I know you are not the children of the Emperor,' the girl said. 'You have been telling us lies.'

Mira closed her eyes. 'Oh brother,' she said.

10

The Ultimate Power

The craftsman's daughter circled her warily. 'I don't know who you are and where you are from, but you are not from the palace.'

'That's true. But please don't get us into trouble. We don't want to cause anyone any harm, really.'

'Are you spies? Thieves?'

'No, we're not. Really we're not.'

'But what are you here for?'

'We have to get something.'

'From the royal chamber in the Necropolis, correct?'

Miranda did not reply.

'So you ARE thieves.'

'No,' she said. 'We don't want to take anything that belongs to the Emperor. We just want to get the cube that Anqi Sheng left. To make it disappear.'

Marko butted in. 'We should just tell her who we are.'

'I was just about to,' said Miranda. 'We're the grandchildren of Anqi Sheng. Only where we come from he has a different name.'

'Yeah,' said Marko, nodding, a serious expression on his face. 'And we don't call him Anqi Sheng. We just call him Grandpa, or Ye-Ye, which is a Chinese nickname kind of thing, meaning the same thing.'

The girl stared at them, not knowing what to believe.

Miranda took hold of Hsiao Ta's hands and spoke as sincerely as she could. 'Look at me—women know when people are lying, right? I'm not lying. You know I'm not. I'm the granddaughter of the man you call Anqi Sheng and he asked us to get the cube back, so that the prophecy can be fulfilled.'

Hsiao Ta asked, 'But what is it?'

Mira looked at her brother and bit her lip. 'This is going to sound really weird,' she said. 'But we don't know. We were just told that we had to go and get it.'

Hsiao Ta released her hands from Miranda's. She walked away. Without turning, she said, 'Can you prove any of this?'

'Look at our clothes,' Marko said. 'Have you ever seen anything like them?'

Hsiao Ta turned and walked back to her friend. She touched the material. 'I have seen nothing like this, not here, nor in the big city. This material is so amazing—finer than the finest silk.'

'Yeah, it's kind of okay, I guess. It's called polyester. Funny how you guys like this stuff. Where we come from, nobody likes it.'

'Show her the locket,' said Marko.

'And there's this,' his sister added. She pulled out the locket. 'This is a picture of our grandfather.'

Hsia Ta looked at the tiny image. 'This is Anqi Sheng?' she said in a gasp. 'It is so real. I have never seen a painting which looked so real.'

Marko smiled. 'Yeah, where we come from the artists are really skilled. We call them photographers. They can paint something like that in a few seconds. In fact, to be technically correct, in one-hundredth of a second. Click. Just like that.'

Miranda spread her palms in a gesture of pleading. 'So have we convinced you? Do you believe we are the grandchildren of a one-thousand-year-old magician?'

Hsiao Ta remained silent.

'Wait,' said Marko. 'Remember the sorcerer talked of the magician having a small vase containing the sun?'

Hsiao Ta's eyes widened.

'I have it in my pocket,' said Marko. 'Come inside, you can appreciate it more.'

The three children ran to one of the tunnel openings and hurried down a ladder into the darkness. Once they were in a place where there was almost no light, Marko spoke again. 'Where are you, Hsiao Ta?'

'I'm here,' came the voice.

'Okay, look in the direction of my voice. I'm going to turn it on. After a countdown of three. Three. Two. One.'

There was a click. But the darkness remained.

'Oops, sorry,' said Marko. 'Let me just try that again. Three. Two. One.'

He clicked the flashlight switch but nothing happened.

Miranda was irritated. 'What are you doing? Can't you turn it on? Here, give it to me.'

'I'm TRYING,' said her brother. 'It's broken. Or run out of batteries. Or something.' She heard him rattling and shaking it. 'It won't come on.'

'Give it to me,' said Miranda.

'NO,' said Marko.

'Give it to ME,' shouted his sister.

'No,' said Hsiao Ta. 'There is no need. Let's go back.'

They heard her moving back towards the tunnel entrance and quickly followed her. As they half-ran along the passage, she explained. 'There's no reason to see the sun in a vase. Your sister is right. Women can tell when people are lying. My mother told me that before she—and you are not lying. I believe you are the children of the children of Anqi Sheng.'

They reached the tunnel entrance that they had entered from, but Hsiao Ta did not move up the ladder. Instead she turned into the darkness in a different direction.

'What are you doing? Are we not going out?' Mira asked.

In the half-light from the tunnel entrance they saw Hsiao Ta, her face serious. 'We are going to a chimney hall where fire is kept burning to collect lanterns,' she said. 'Then we are going to the forbidden chamber. There you will meet the ghost brigade, if you so wish. I do not promise that you will enjoy the experience.'

***

As they walked, Hsiao Ta told them about the Emperor and his family.

'The Emperor is a cruel man. Everybody knows that.

When we first heard of him, he seemed to be such a great hero. He united all the countries into one and became the ruler of all. The first Emperor of all the civilised lands in the world. One people under heaven—that's what we said he had achieved.'

'All countries?' said Miranda. 'Not ours.'

'If you are from Mount Penglai, that is also in our kingdom, on its very edge. And there are other lands, they say, beyond the seas, but they are manned only by savages, not fully human.'

Marko said, 'So he was a hero at first?'

'Yes. But slowly things changed. He became evil. He became cruel and harsh. He killed one advisor and then another and another. Then last year, he did something that shocked everybody. He killed the intellectuals. He killed 460 writers and scientists. Many said they were the wisest people in the kingdom.'

Hsiao Ta's face became heavy and she looked down. They could see tears swimming in her eyes.

Miranda said: 'Your mother?'

The girl nodded. 'She was the first woman alchemist. And probably the last.'

Marko asked, 'Did anyone try to stop him?'

'No one dared. Who would dare to criticise someone who

kills his friends, let alone his enemies? But then, one day, one person did stand up to him.'

'Fusu, his oldest son,' said the boy, excitedly. 'I read about him in Grandpa's history book.'

Hsiao Ta nodded. 'His oldest son, Fusu, was a good and fearless man.'

Miranda said, 'And probably the only person that the Emperor would not kill for criticising him—he wouldn't kill his own family members, would he?'

Hsiao Ta turned to her, her face stern. 'You know so little. You need education. He killed many members of his own family, including children he had fathered. Many of his wives and concubines try to get as far away from him as possible. Which is why at first I was not surprised when you knew so little about palace life.'

Marko said, 'But he didn't kill his son. What with him being, like first-born, heir to the throne kind of thing.'

Hsia Ta turned to him. 'No. He banished him. He sent him to work in the far part of the kingdom, where he could cause no trouble. Instead, he made his brother, Huhai, his heir. This is a great tragedy for the kingdom. Because Huhai is just like his father. Hard and cruel.'

They walked in silence for a while.

Miranda said, 'Tonight is a very important night. We

have a way of knowing when important things are going to happen, and it tells us that everything changes tonight. It's kind of hard to explain.'

Suddenly an adult male voice spoke. 'Change may be good. Or it may be bad.'

The three children, startled, spun on their heels.

Craftsman Tang stepped out of the shadows. 'I heard your voices. These tunnels echo a great deal. Sound travels.'

Miranda got the message. He was warning them to keep their secrets more tightly to their chests.

The man continued speaking. 'You are right when you say that tonight is a special night. Rumour has it that there is going to be a meeting between father and son tonight. The Emperor has left the palace. He is on the road. He will meet Fusu. If they do meet, we can only hope that there will be a reconciliation, that the Emperor will realise that what he did was wrong, and Fusu's criticism came out of love and kindness. But there are other rumours—which tell a different story.'

Hsiao Ta looked at her father but said nothing.

'What are they?' Marko asked in a nervous whisper.

'The other rumour says that the Emperor will hand his son a death paper.'

Hsiao Ta gulped and dropped her eyes. 'That would be bad.'

'Wait,' said Miranda. 'What is a death paper?'

Tang said, 'There are many leaders who can order people to be put to death. There have been many in history. But this Emperor wants to show that he is more powerful than any who have gone before. He wishes to be seen as a god. So he writes notes ordering people to kill themselves.'

Miranda's eyes were wide. 'And do they?'

Tang nodded. 'They do.'

'But why?' Marko asked.

'It is the ultimate power. The Emperor wants power over more than just the bodies of his people. He wants power over the will of his people. To kill someone takes nothing but a few soldiers. But to order people to kill themselves and have that order followed, that is the greatest power that a man can have. Power over the human will.'

Marko shook his head. 'This guy is a MAJOR baddie,' he said, folding his arms. 'I wish I hadn't pretended to be his son.'

As they stepped into the light, they became aware of a great commotion that was going on.

Craftsman Tang grabbed the shoulder of one of the men running past. 'What's happening? Why all the noise?'

The man turned to him, fear in his eyes. 'We have an unexpected visitor,' he said. 'The Minister of Justice is here.'

Tang let the man go, and he disappeared as fast as he could.

Marko asked, 'Minister of Justice? Is he a good guy? That's the sort of title a good guy should have!'

Tang looked serious. 'He is not, as you say, a good guy. Li Si is the most dangerous man in the kingdom—the king's personal killer.'

'Eww,' said Miranda. 'You mean, like, he's an executioner?'

The craftsman shook his head. 'No. If you get sent to the executioner, you count yourself lucky. That's far better than being sent to Li Si, who is the Chancellor of Fear. He is a master in the art of pain. They call him Slow Death.'

Mira and Marko had been stepping steadily backwards while Tang spoke. They wanted to get as far away from the new arrival as possible.

Then they heard the clattering of hooves and a cloud of dust rose in the air to their left. Four horsemen appeared out of the dust and came straight towards the small group and quickly surrounded them.

Hsiao Ta hid behind her father, while Mira and Marko stood in front of him.

The largest of the four men spoke. 'The Minister of Justice wishes to see the two thieves who have been pretending to be the children of his divine highness, the Emperor. They are to be executed immediately.'

'They are just children,' Tang said. 'Playing a game. They are not thieves.'

The man on horseback glared at him. 'You say one more word, craftsman, and you will suffer the same fate.'

Two men dismounted and slung chains around Miranda and Marko.

'This is not good,' Marko said. 'Think of something.'

'That's your job,' his sister replied.

11

The Chancellor of Fear

They were taken by guards to the palace of the man they called Slow Death and left outside.

Half an hour later, guards came and dragged them in by their chains.

Slow Death was a rake-thin man with a clear complexion and soft features. He wore long pale yellow robes, ornately embroidered with purple thread. He spoke quietly, almost in a whisper, but his eyes were hard and cruel.

'What's that bag thing on the boy's back?' he asked.

The guards pulled Marko's backpack away from him.

At first, they couldn't work out how to undo the zip, but by tugging at the bag in various directions, the zip eventually slid down. One guard, a man with a flat nose and a jutting chin, pulled out the Magic Mirror of the Moon.

The Chancellor of Fear gestured to the man to bring it over. 'I've heard about these,' he said in his soft drawl. 'A magic mirror. Made of a special bronze alloy, so I hear. Very valuable. Very unusual properties. Who did you steal it from?' This last phrase was loud and harsh.

'It belongs to our grandfather, Anqi Sheng,' said Miranda.

Marko was nervous about most things, but the mirror was one thing he would fiercely fight for—because the thing he was most scared about was losing the mirror and not being able to return to the present day. 'Give it back,' the boy said. 'It's ours.'

Li Si looked it over on both sides. 'Just a piece of nicely carved junk,' he said, his voice quiet and calm again. 'Now, shall I drop you two in the vat, or drop your little trinket in?'

The two children looked up at the cruel man. What did he mean? What was he talking about? What was the vat?

Li Si turned to the guard. He said, 'Drop it into vat number seven. That's bronze alloy and we could do with a bit more there.'

'Give it back,' Marko barked.

The Minister of Justice, suddenly barked at the top of his voice: 'Evil thieves! Your little trinket is going to be melted down, just over there. You can watch if you like.'

He gestured to one of his staff members to pull open the doors of the palace. They saw the soldier march to the foundry outside where furnaces roared and vats of molten metal stood. The soldier tossed the disk up to one of the workers with a shout.

The man grabbed the mirror and glanced at it.

The soldier, unable to shout over the roar of the flames, pointed to the vat and then pointed back to the palace of Li Si. The message was clear. The Emperor's envoy wanted the magic mirror thrown into the molten metal vat to be melted into nothing.

'No,' shouted Marko.

But it was too late. The man dropped the magic mirror. The white hot bubbling liquid fizzed slightly and swallowed it up.

Marko froze in horror.

Miranda, on one of the very rare occasions of her life, was completely silent.

'Bye bye, little trinket,' said Li Si sweetly. The man seemed to constantly swing between towering rage and absolute tranquillity. This made him even more terrifying.

The Minister of Justice turned to the guards who were still in the room. 'Take these two brats and hand them over to the ghost brigade.'

The guards froze, suddenly nervous.

'What's wrong?' said Li Si. 'Did you not hear me?'

'Yes, sir,' said the guards, still looking scared.

Li Si added, 'And go back an hour later for the corpses. We must tidy up after ourselves. Keep the Necropolis clean.'

***

Marko didn't speak for over ten minutes. He just walked in silence, gazing into the middle distance. This was a problem as far as Mira was concerned, since she badly needed his help in working out what they were going to do.

She remembered her favourite teacher, Ms Modi, saying that super-imaginative children often worried more than other children about things, since they could picture all the bad things that could happen in terrifying detail, whereas ordinary children could just get on with things.

Mira really *really* wanted to take some sort of drastic action. She and Marko were being frog-marched along the hall to the entrance to the ghost arena. They either needed to break free and run off—difficult since they had guards on either side of them—or they needed to stay put and allow themselves to be taken to the place where the ghosts were.

They needed to go to the entrance to the Emperor's burial room.

And then there were bigger questions to deal with. One was: how to stop the ghosts killing them once they were there? And if they survived that, how to get home without the magic mirror? Moonlight shining through the mirror was the only way they knew of transporting themselves between their usual world and the world they were in at the moment.

Suddenly, Marko spoke. 'It's gone,' he murmured, toneless as a zombie.

'It's gone,' she agreed.

'We lost it.' He said nothing for a while, and then, in the same toneless voice, said, 'Oops.'

For some reason, this annoyed her. 'Oops? Did you say "oops"?'

He nodded.

'The mirror, our only chance of getting back to our own time and place is gone, and you say OOPS?'

'Well, it is a bit of a downer, isn't it? We'll never get home. Never ever ever. We'll be stuck here for ever and ever. And ever and ever. Et cetera.'

'*Downer*? That's almost as bad as oops!'

'Bummer?'

'Shut up.'

'Well you get angry at anything I say but you don't say anything yourself.'

'Because I don't have an intelligent functioning person with a brain to say it to. I only have you, my half-wit brother. It is not a bit of a downer. It's a tragedy. It's a nightmare. It's horrible. It's ... it's ... it's a DISASTER. We'll never see our parents again. We'll never see our friends again. We'll never see our house again. I'll miss the end-of-year school disco.'

He nodded. 'I know. If we had to get stuck somewhere in time, it's a pity it's here. I mean, there have been lots of emperors and kings and stuff, but I can't think of many who did more killing of his own people than this one.'

They reached the tunnel entrance. Miranda said, 'Unfortunately, we may be next on the list, unless we can think of something pretty darn quick.'

***

'On the orders of the Minister of Justice, these two are to be fed to the ghost brigade,' the soldier barked to Craftsman Tang.

'They're just children. They won't last a minute.'

The soldiers glared at him.

'May I suggest—'

'No,' barked the larger of the two soldiers. 'You may not

suggest anything. The orders are to deliver these two to the ghost brigade and collect their corpses afterwards.'

'Okay,' said Craftsman Tang. 'Follow me.'

They pulled the chains off the children—metal was valuable, and could not be wasted on junior corpses. They walked down a pitch-dark tunnel lit by candles in sconces on the walls. They got to a large wooden door, which he unlocked with two keys.

He carried a lit torch through the darkness down another tunnel, this one unlit, until they reached another wooden door. This one had to be opened with three keys. The blackness and silence were oppressive, and the tunnel was becoming increasingly creepy.

'How far now?' said one of the soldiers, a trace of nervousness creeping into his voice.

'We have another passage before we get to the area where the ghosts roam. Of course sometimes they come out of that area and go quite a long way down these tunnels, so be careful.'

'What do you mean they get out?' said the soldier, coming to a sudden halt. 'How far do they come?'

'About this far,' said Tang.

The soldier made a decision. 'We'll stay here. You take them into the final room.'

'Very well.'

Craftsman Tang moved away with the two children. Since he had the torch, the two soldiers were soon left in the dark.

'Wait,' said one of the soldiers. 'Come back. You leave us the torch. You can go ahead in the dark.'

Tang turned back and handed the torch to the soldiers. Then he and the children moved forward into the dark.

They were soon lost to view.

'Wait,' they heard the soldier say again. 'We can't see you.'

Craftsman Tang replied with infinite patience in his voice. 'You can't see us because you have the torch. If you want to see us, give us the torch.'

'We're keeping the torch,' said the soldier.

'Right,' said his companion. 'We're keeping the torch.'

Tang said that they would stomp loudly on the floor to prove that they were heading away from there. 'You'll hear our feet as we move away, getting quieter. Then you'll hear me unlocking the final door, pushing the children in, and then relocking the door. Then you'll hear me coming back alone. Then I will return to you and we will go back to the world of the living together. Is that all right?'

'Yes. Just do it. Now. And be quick,' said the soldier.

There was silence except for the shuffling of feet as Tang and the two children headed into the final passage.

Tang whispered to them, 'I'll try to make enough noise for all three of us. You two sneak back. Go quietly. Flatten yourselves against the wall on the right. Sneak past the soldiers.'

'Won't the men see us when we get close to them?' Miranda whispered.

Tang said, 'No. I gave them a weak torch. It'll go out very soon. They'll be waiting in the dark.'

The craftsman's plan worked like a dream. Within minutes, the soldiers' torch had gone out and the two men were standing in the dark.

The two children sneaked back and went right past them.

Miranda, feeling wicked, gave a tiny high-pitched howl as she passed by them.

'What was that?' said one of the men. 'It sounded like a ghost.'

'I heard it too,' said the other. 'And it's close to us.'

Marko blew in the direction of the voices.

'Did you feel that? It's breathing. It's behind us,' said the other.

The two children got to the wooden door, swung it open

and entered the next passage, resisting the temptation to laugh at the terrified soldiers in the dark behind them.

'Keep going,' Miranda whispered to Marko. 'When the soldiers get too scared, they'll run out of the passage in this direction, and we want to be well clear by then.'

They reached the final door just as they heard the soldiers approaching. The men had clearly reached their limit of endurance.

Mira and Marko raced through the dark and found the final door. They yanked it open and had to shield their eyes against the brightness.

Miranda blinked. She heard her brother say: 'Uh oh.'

She opened her eyes wider. There were several men standing in their way. And they carried gleaming torches. Right in front was the Prince of Pain.

'Well, well, well,' said the Minister of Justice, in his creepy quiet voice. 'Look what we have here. I rather suspected that those idiots would not be up to the job, so I decided that I would come and make sure the job was done properly, myself. And what a good thing I did.'

12

The Ghost Arena

Ten minutes later, Miranda and Marko were thrown into the ghost arena. The door slammed behind them. There was a sound in the dark, supposedly empty chamber. And then came a whistling noise. A crossbow bolt thudded into the door behind them.

Marko squealed and flattened himself against the floor.

'The ghosts are awake. We'll take your bodies out later,' said Li Si's lieutenant, his voice muffled by the thick wooden door. 'Your souls can join those of the ghosts in this chamber.'

The two children lay in silence, not daring to move.

For five minutes, nothing happened.

Then a ghost spoke. 'Mira,' it said, the voice distant and like an echo. 'Mira, can you hear me?'

She didn't answer.

Her brother spoke in a matter-of-fact way. 'The ghost is talking to you.'

'I know. I can hear it,' she whispered, tremulously.

'Well, shouldn't you answer?'

'NO! I'm not going to answer. You KNOW why I'm not going to answer. It's a GHOST. It's my policy not to answer ghosts.'

He thought for a moment. 'Is that a new policy or has that always been your policy?'

'Mira,' said the ghostly voice again. 'It's Hsiao Ta. If you can hear me, shout.'

'What? Hsiao Ta? You're the ghost?'

'You can hear me?'

'Yes, we can hear you. Where are you? Is it all right to talk loudly like this? Speaking won't anger the ghosts?'

'There are no ghosts.'

'Then who was shooting at us?'

'They are automatic crossbows. My father's brother made them. It took him weeks. He's rather proud of them.'

Marko spoke. 'Where are you? How come we can hear you?'

'They made us build a network of speaking tubes into parts of the Necropolis. They didn't tell us why. But there could be a lot of reasons.'

Marko looked at Miranda. He whispered to her, 'It's so they can communicate with them after they have locked them in to starve to death. It said so in Grandpa's history book.'

'Shh. They don't know any of that.'

'Shouldn't we tell them?'

'I think maybe they can guess.' Miranda looked up and called to the ceiling, speaking to Hsiao Ta, 'How do we get out of here?'

'My uncle's on his way here. He'll tell you. Be patient. And whatever you do, don't move.'

'Don't worry. We're not going anywhere.'

Five minutes later, they heard a deeper voice coming through the speaking tube.

'Hello, Mira and Marko. I'm Tang Xi Lim, Hsiao Ta's uncle. There are tripwires at irregular intervals throughout the darkest parts of the tunnel system. Touch one, even lightly, and the crossbows will be triggered.'

'Okay. We got that.'

'Lie on the ground. Don't move.'

This admonition was followed by silence.

Mira was annoyed. 'Is that the advice you are going to give us? Lie on the ground and don't move? What happens after the first month of lying on the ground and not moving?'

The man spoke again. 'I'm just looking through my floor plan. Lie on the ground and then crawl sideways, not forward. Go to your left. It's important that you don't go forward.'

Marko spoke, 'Can't we do something like in *Mission Impossible* where he goes along the ceiling?'

'They don't have *Mission Impossible* here. He won't know what you're talking about,' his sister said.

'I was talking to you, not him.' Marko raised his voice to talk to Tang Xi Lim. 'Can we go along the ceiling somehow? The roof?'

'You cannot. Unless you are a spider. There is nothing up there but clean rock. Not for the first hundred metres anyway. Then there are the lights.'

'Lights?' Marko pondered. 'How can they have light fittings in this period of history?'

'So what do we do?' Miranda asked. 'Crawl sideways, you said?'

'Yes, crawl sideways. You will reach the side wall. There should be no tripwires on that part. Then stand close to the wall, and reach up. There is a sort of scaffolding fixed to the wall. It runs the length of the tunnel. It provides the fixing gantries for the crossbows. If you can climb up to that scaffolding, then you can proceed through the tunnel to the royal death chamber without being shot. But you must be careful.'

'Will the gantry hold our weight?'

'It will. It is built to hold grown men. I have seen you. You two together will barely equal the weight of one man.'

'If we shake it, will the crossbows go off?'

'They will. It is inevitable. As you proceed down the tunnel, you will shake the mechanisms. The crossbows will be triggered. The bolts will be fired. But they will be fired through the centre of the tunnel. If you are up on the sidewalls, high enough, you should be unharmed. But be careful. The bolts ricochet off the walls and can go in any direction.'

Miranda heard a shuffling sound. Marko was shuffling forward on his tummy, like a snake. 'Let's go,' he said.

Less than five minutes later, they were both perched on a tiny platform on the wall of the tunnel. Marko had climbed up first. When Miranda had joined him, the gantry had swung slightly and they heard the click and swoosh of a crossbow bolt being fired. Then they heard it thud twice.

'It's hitting the wall somewhere and ricocheting off, like the guy said,' said Marko. 'It's dangerous around here.'

They carefully shuffled forward.

It took them ten minutes to get all the way through the ghost tunnel.

As they reached the end of it, they could see a glow, which gradually turned into a steady light. They had reached the Emperor's burial room. After receiving assurances of safety, they hopped down. Tang Xi Lim had told them that there were no automatic crossbows in this part of the complex.

The light came from a network of what looked like bulbs in the ceiling. Of course they couldn't be lights in the modern sense—the children knew that. Miranda assumed they must be a network of channels that led to the open air.

'They must be like my remote viewer,' said Marko. 'A network of periscopes—that sort of thing.'

They had expected a coffin, but instead there was a solid gold chair in front of a huge undulating area of glowing land.

'What is that?' Marko asked, pointing to the strange shapes in the ground. It was hard to see in the poorly lit room.

'I think it's a map,' his sister replied. 'I think it's supposed to be the country the Emperor is going to rule after he's dead. Remember how they said that the king believed that representations grow to full size?'

'It's like Legoland,' said the boy, recalling a miniature kingdom that the two of them had visited with their parents when they were younger.

As their eyes became more accustomed to the dark, they realised that the map was crisscrossed with glowing rivers. They were like flowing streams of silver.

'Wow, look at that,' said Mira. 'Rivers of mercury. It's amazing.'

The room seemed to shimmer with a network of stars set in the ceiling, and the surreal glowing landscape in front of the throne.

But she was snapped out of her reverie by the thought that they had a mission to complete. 'Where's the cube?' she asked.

'There,' said Marko. 'It's under the Emperor's chair.'

They pulled it out.

It was simply a large wooden cube, about the size of a microwave oven, but squarer. There was nothing special about it. It had no hinges, no line which suggested a lid, no latch of any kind.

'It's just a cube of wood,' she said, disappointed. 'What's special about it?'

Marko gently took it from her hands.

She snatched it back. 'Don't snatch,' she said.

'I just want to see how heavy it is,' he said. 'See if there's something inside. Maybe it's like those puzzle boxes Grandpa has at home.'

'That's an idea.'

They put the box down and started prodding and poking it.

Both of them had spent many hours learning how to open Grandpa's collection of Oriental puzzle boxes. Eventually, Marko had an idea.

'Because it's so big, I think it'll need two of us to do it,' he said. 'You hold it still with your hand at the back and the top, and I'll try to slide the side open, like in box number one in Grandpa's study.'

They tried it several times, but nothing happened.

Then they tried the pattern for the second box in Grandpa's study. Again, there was no result. But the third time they got lucky. Finally! It slid open like a dream.

'Great,' said Miranda. 'Now let's see what's in it.'

They opened it. Inside was a mirror.

'It's another magic mirror,' she said.

'No it isn't. It's OUR magic mirror. Look at the markings on the sides. It's our mirror.'

'But how can that be? It was just destroyed.'

'I don't know. And I can't be bothered to think about it. I'm too busy feeling happy. Marko, we're going home.'

They both shouted a spontaneous yelp of delight. 'Yippeee!'

'And where is your home?' a deep voice asked.

They turned, surprised to see a dark figure in the corner of the room.

He stepped into a shaft of light.

13

The Tomb of Time

Chief Architect General Meng stepped into the room. Behind him stood Craftsman Tang.

The architect spoke. 'We offered to come and collect your dead bodies. Tang told me that it would be safe—and that I would find you alive and well. I understand you claim to be the children of Anqi Sheng.'

'Grandchildren,' said Marko. 'To be precise.'

'That is a big claim to make—to be the offspring of a thousand-year-old magician.'

The boy shrugged his shoulders. The movement caused

his malfunctioning flashlight to fall out of his pocket. It hit the floor, and turned itself on. A beam of light shone to the ceiling.

Craftsman Tang took a step back. 'The vase of sunshine? The sorcerer spoke of this.'

General Meng looked down at the flashlight. His jaw dropped open.

Marko picked it up and gave it a shake and a thump. He turned it on and off a couple of times. 'Thank goodness it's working again. Must have been a loose connection somewhere. Must open it up and have a look at the insides when I get the chance.' He realised that he was becoming more independent. Until now, if something had broken, he would have assumed that it would be the duty of one of the adults in the house to fix it.

'Are you here to steal the Emperor's property?' This was General Meng.

'No,' said Miranda. 'We're here to fulfil the prophecy. That the cube would disappear to mark the moment when everything changes. When the Emperor dies, I mean, moves from normal life to whatever comes next.'

The General shook his head. 'We just received news of the Emperor from the Minister of Justice. The sorcerer has for several weeks been giving him a special potion that will enable our leader to live far longer than a normal man. Twice or thrice as long.'

'Hang on,' said Marko. 'What is this special potion? We don't even have stuff that does that where we come from, and we have loads of cool stuff you don't have.'

The architect said, 'They are made of one of the most rare and magical substances on earth. Liquid metal. Quicksilver. It has many names. Mercury. You see it flowing in the rivers there.'

He pointed to the shining rivers of molten metal flowing through the scale map of the Necropolis.

'Uh oh,' said Marko.

Miranda said, 'If the Emperor has been taking mercury for several weeks, then I have news for you. The Emperor is going to die soon, very soon.'

General Meng and Craftsman Tang stared at each other.

Marko nodded. 'Yeah, she's right. It's a deadly poison.'

His sister asked, 'Where is Hsiao Ta? We have to speak to her.'

'She's gone,' said Craftsman Tang.

'Can you get her?

'No, she's gone. Gone forever. She didn't feel safe here. She's gone to join the child army. They've left—they've started their journey to the sea. She said she felt safer with the sorcerer than she did here.' Miranda said, 'She may be right. I don't know. You're not safe anywhere. As soon as the Emperor is dead, the Minister of Justice is going to seal all of the craftsmen in the tomb. You'll die here.'

The two men looked at each other again. Tang said, 'It may be that the Emperor is already dead. That would explain the unexpected visit of the Minister of Justice. Come, we must go.'

The four of them raced through the tunnel. The two men knew a long network of secret passages that led them to the edge of the encampment, emerging in some woods.

Miranda bit her bottom lip. 'I do hope Hsiao Ta will be safe.'

'I trust the sorcerer,' said Craftsman Tang. 'After all, if what you say is true, he has rid us of our lethal Emperor and escaped with a large group of people.'

Two children ran to a clearing in the woods with the magic mirror and waited for the moon to rise. It was time to go home.

***

The sun shone through the classroom window.

The history teacher, an elderly woman named Stella Sims, sat at her desk, packing pens and paper into a bag. It was break-time, and the sound of children playing could be heard through the half-open windows.

There was a knock on the door. She looked up.

Miranda and Marko Lee entered the room.

'Well, hello there,' she said. 'My favourite pupils.' She gave them a quizzical look. 'Are you just visiting for social reasons, or is there something I can do for you?'

'Can we ask you a question?' the girl asked.

'Of course.'

'You know the ship of young people, the children's army that the magician guy took to Mount Penglai?'

Mrs Sims took a moment to understand what Miranda was talking about. 'Are you referring to the expeditions of the first Emperor of China's sorcerer, back in—when was it—210 BC?'

Marko nodded. 'We want to know what happened to the ship of young people. One of our friends is on it.'

His sister glared at him. 'WAS on it,' she said. 'It was like two thousand years ago.'

'I know, but it doesn't feel so long ago,' he said. 'Time flies and all that.'

Mrs Sims smiled. She was used to the fact that these two youngsters appeared to live in a fantasy world, where history and modern life intermingled. It was great that they had such an active imagination, especially considering the superb grades they got in History as a result.

'What happened to the three thousand teenagers?'

Miranda continued. 'When the sorcerer took his second expedition to look for the Mount of the Gods, he took three thousand teenagers with them? To find the elixir of life?'

'Oh yes, I do remember this,' said the history teacher. 'Let me think. Some people called it the ship of virgins, since all the young people were unmarried. The first Emperor's sorcerer, what was his name?'

'Xufu,' said Marko.

'That's right, Xufu. On his final journey he took a huge fleet of ships with several thousand soldiers and several thousand young people.'

'To find Anqi Sheng on the island of Immortals,' Miranda said. 'What we want to know is this: did they sacrifice the young people?'

'Yeah,' said her brother. 'Did they throw them overboard? Or kill them some other way?'

The history teacher scratched her chin, trying to recall what the latest research said.

'Well, no one knows the exact details of what happened—after all, we are talking about something that happened two millennia ago. But if I remember correctly, none of the legends talk about them killing the youngsters—quite the contrary in fact.' She smiled.

'What do you mean by that?' Miranda asked.

'I don't think they lost their lives. The majority of sources said the opposite. I mean, they were fruitful and multiplied.'

This baffled her audience.

'Translation?' Miranda asked.

The history teacher leaned back in her chair and intertwined the fingers of her hands. 'The legend says that the sorcerer knew the Emperor was a mad monster who would eventually kill him, since the elixir of immortality did not exist. So he put a plan into motion—to escape and start a new country. And, some say, that's exactly what he did.'

Miranda's eyebrows rose. 'He started a new country?'

'Yes. He sailed across the Bay of Bohai and the Yellow Sea and out into the Pacific Ocean. He landed on a beautiful island and settled his people there. With lots of young people they established a colony. The teenage boys and teenage girls married each other, eventually had children, and a new country was formed.'

'Where was the island?'

'Nobody knows for sure which one it was. Some scholars think that the sorcerer and the Ship of Youngsters landed on the northwest coast of Japan. Certainly Japan had few inhabitants in those days, and did suddenly expand in population from about that period onwards. So that may have been it. Or they may have landed somewhere else. As you know, there are a great many islands along the coast of the Pacific Ocean—several thousand.'

'Thank God,' said Miranda. 'Now I can stop worrying about her. Er, my friend who was on that ship. Two thousand years ago.'

Mrs Sims smiled. 'You guys have a powerful imagination. Anyway, I have a better idea. Now that you know you don't have to worry about your friend, why not instead go and make plans to visit her descendants? A trip to Japan could be fun.'

Minutes later, they were walking down the school corridor, heading to the playground. But Marko turned left to go to the library instead. 'Where are you going?' his sister asked.

'When we got back last night from 210 BC, there was a new mark on the magic mirror. On the edge. There are three marks there now. I'm going to go and look them up. I'm sure they mean something.'

The girl nodded. There were still many mysteries to unravel. The footsteps they had heard in their home, which had prompted their journey to the land of the first Emperor of China, remained a mystery. On their return they had searched the house, but found it empty.

Miranda thought about joining Marko in the library, but then noticed a cluster of her friends at the end of the corridor.

One of them, a tall, dark girl called Melani Sun, smiled at her. 'Hi, Mira,' she said. 'We're just talking about what to wear for the end-of-year school disco. My dad said he'd pay for a new outfit for me if I read three books in a week, and I'm halfway through the third.'

'Cool,' said Miranda. 'You know what I'm thinking?'

'What?'

'I'm thinking I might wear something from your mom's shop.'

The girls' mouths dropped open.

Melani said, 'You mean that polyester print stuff that my mom sells?'

'Yeah. I actually think it's kinda cool in a retro sort of way.'

To her delight, the girls nodded. 'Could be,' said Melani. 'If you chose really carefully. My mom would be so thrilled if it came back into fashion.'

Miranda continued: 'There's something special about it. It's soft and smooth, fit for the daughter of an Emperor in my book.'

A Note From The Authors

Although this book is classified as a novel, it's full of true events—and some of the most unbelievable things in it are taken straight from the works of historians!

There really was an emperor named Qin Shi Huang who wanted to live forever, and he did all the things that this book says he did. He claimed to have met a thousand-year-old magician called Anqi Sheng, and he put to death hundreds of alchemists who failed to give him the potion he wanted. And he really did die in 210 after taking mercury.

There really was a court sorcerer named Xufu who was given the job of finding Mount Penglai, and ancient legends say he sailed away with thousands of young people, and landed on an island where they started a new country.

And there really was a Necropolis, just as it's been described in this book. It was lost for more than 2000 years, but was found again in the 1970s. Even today, you can visit a place in China called Xian, where you can see the soldiers that Craftsman Tang made, you can see the man-made mountain that was built for the Emperor, and you can see the remains of the ruler's huge tomb.

Even some of the more eyebrow-raising details in this book, such as the ghost brigade of automatic crossbows, the underground chariots, the water realm, the storyteller with the faraway look in his eyes, and so on—are all taken from real life.

And most amazing of all, the magic mirror itself is something you can see examples of in museums, as several have survived right up to modern days.

We hope you enjoyed this book. We had great fun writing it. There are lots of different books in this series. Collect them all and you can learn a lot about our amazing past.

Magic Mirror #3 the Tomb of Time

MODEL: The First Emperor's Soldiers
Scale Height = 15mm

Legend

- Cut / Fold / Glue
- Mountain (concave fold)
- Valley (convex fold)

STEP 1.

Cut out soldiers, cavalry and chariots around the edges as shown below, leaving the blue areas so figures are more stable when folded.

STEP 2.

Fold mountain and valley folds as indicated with earth tone bases upwards. Glue figure standups.

Bend chariot roof to match curve of chariot sides, and fold ends with glue tabs as indicated.

V
M
V
M
V
V
M
V
M
M
V
M
V
V
V
M
M

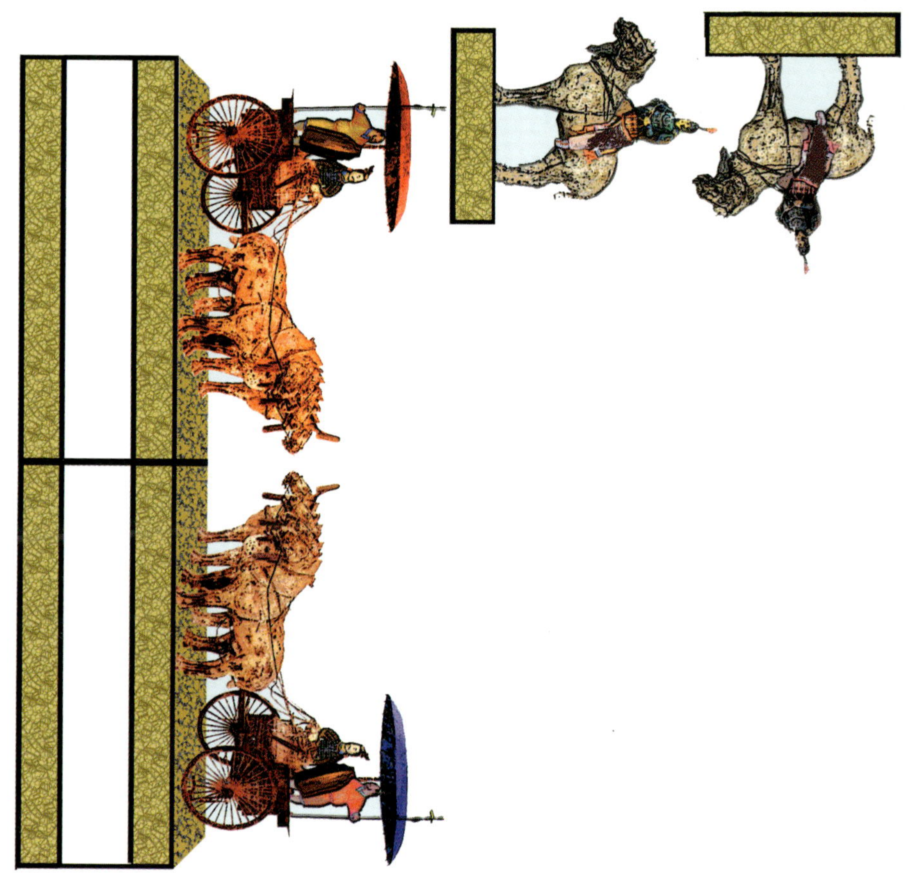